Means to Be Lucky

Means to Be Lucky

Poems and Translations

Annie Kantar

Cover image: Stephen Reichert, *Crowd Sourced Beauty*, 2019. Oil on canvas, 38" x 54".

Published 2023 in New York by Poets & Traitors Press
www.poets-traitors.com
poetstraitors@gmail.com

Editors: Val Vinokur, Anna Scola

Published in the United States of America.

Poets & Traitors Press is an independent publisher of books of poetry and translations by a single author/translator. The press emerged from the Poet/Translator Reading Series and from the New School's Literary Translation Workshop to showcase authors who travel between writing and translation, artists for whom Language is made manifest through languages and whose own word carries, shapes, and is shaped by that of another.

Poets & Traitors Press acknowledges support from Eugene Lang College, the New School Bachelor's Program for Adults and Transfer Students, and the New School Foreign Languages Department.

ISBN: 978-0-9990737-6-6

for my parents

Means to Be Lucky

CONTENTS

iii.

FOREWORD

If she's lucky, much of a poet's time is spent alone: alone with her ear, alone with the images she's beginning to discern, alone in her abiding intuitions and affinities in a place she loves, a changing place that changes her. Alone with the questions she's been brooding over longer than she can remember. Paradoxically, it's also here, in solitude, that she registers something of what it means to be hospitable. A word whose Latin roots trace back to *hospes*, meaning guest, stranger and host at once, to be hospitable is to feel at home and make another feel the same among the very real energies and sensibilities that surround her—sometimes clearly her own, sometimes mysteriously other.

Perhaps the poet-translator understands better than anybody the experience of inhabiting, and sometimes, being inhabited by, a place into which she was welcomed as guest, or even a stranger. In the poem she's translating, the translator finds rooms she can see inside and others she can't, from which, say, sounds and movement emerge. She finds conversation, that is, a turning back together—to the liveliness and intimacy of the moment at hand. As much as what's being said, how it's said—the delicate interactions between words and their meanings, sounds and silences—are sources of joy and even fascination. "Maybe / what's farthest off of all / will restore my soul," is how the great modern Hebrew poet Leah Goldberg put it in her poem, "Day Off." Anyone who's felt the absorbing force of deep hospitality will know what I mean.

It goes without saying that something similar happens for a poet translating, so to speak, her "own" experience, directly in her "own" language, in her "own" poem. From a serendipitous alchemy of hard work and surrender, she's crafting a world—

even, or especially, when that world is hard to find elsewhere. In the best cases, these moments are a little like prayer: someone is listening, someone the poet doesn't know, who knows her better than she knows herself. And still, how, when, or whether the poem will come to be is anyone's guess. What's for certain in those hours is that words and the relationships they forge between and beyond each other matter.

At bottom, this relational sensibility rests, perhaps naively, on the belief that caring for language is a way of caring for the world, that attending to words and their letters might unlock secrets, set things right. In some small but crucial measure, as guests, strangers and hosts, our lives are ongoing translations— of what's been given, and of givenness itself. That givenness is the rich and contingent physical world that time and again arouses amazement. Most palpable for me in that amazement is less a distanced sense of awe than an often bewildering feeling of involvement and desire to respond.

How to live in this world that asks so much of us, and gives so much more back? How to welcome—and ultimately, honor— the natural, human and (if I may) supernatural sources of my amazement? What are my responsibilities? The ethical challenges inherent in these questions are obvious, but feel ever acute in Jerusalem, where I've spent most of my adult life. Behind the poems in this collection and translations I've placed in conversation with them is the sense that I'm a guest in a world that *deserves* attention and tending-to. The chance to dwell among these questions with others is the better part of what, for me, it means to be lucky.

The depths must be hidden. But where? On the surface.

- Hugo von Hofmannsthal

Means to Be Lucky

i.

A CONVERGENCE

A mark,

    a language, a token,

        an omen,

portent,

    how it's said,

    might come

down to *con-*

        stellation, significant,

or Sanskrit: *to see,*

        look, seek.

        ~

A pity no one can truly

trace how things *rhyme,*
        that is, *get along*

    symmetrically or in proportion,

move or flow—it depends (I guess)

on providence,

fortune or grace—though

the fact that things
can,

and do, seems

to me a mystery

meant for multitudes.

~

In Hebrew a sign's *siman*,

an omen

of an apple,

carrot, honey, beetroot we

ingest to usher in the new,

hoping to remember

words are multiple,

multi-pull—

in meaning, never to be

just one

to take in or become

~

Human:
        (featherless planti-

grade biped
        mammal) which

is to suffer
Cf. *allow to occur,*

        continue, fail
to prevent or suppress)

        such that the sufferer is
he, or she, on either side

        of that equation:
a painful *condition,*

agreed upon.

~

Though experts are
                              divided as to a *victim's* origins.

Some suggest sacrifice as

it bears resemblance to *vicis* (turn,
occasion). Connected

perhaps by *viscous*

                    bodily fluids,

vicious droplets,

                    what happens to you happens, too,

to me (powers-that-be

                    dislike this fact

                              of biology)...

                         ~

Coming down, perhaps, to this:

          no one's ever
                    just that

one but rather,

in exchange with

knobs and branches

along paths where

people link

up at the edges, scent to scent,

body to body.

~

And naturally, mind to

mind— which meant
loving memory.

Someone long ago thought, populonia—

she who protects against devastation—

and:

people.

I've wanted to share

the source of a certain despair

but nothing stays

in place. Somehow, the mind

is where we love

what's gone. Roots *(underground*

part of a plant) turn

to trunks.

A word meaning *body* has

replaced *life* in certain

tongues. Wherever

we look, the wonder of seeing—

to behold in the imagination, or a dream—

in a word, what we mean.

THE ORIGINS OF USELESS THINGS

For nothing,
says the rose from its root.

For you alone, says
the pomegranate.

*Something inside will
burst for naught—*

But what does it do?
My oh my o mine,

the sound of the earth
in the wind's hair . . .

CLING OF THE WORLD

What could it mean
to imagine you,
then try to make ourselves
into one we believe
would please you?

What could that be,
and what is it to be,
and what good is
it to know what
it means, virtue?

You see, you
confuse this
ordinary Jew who trusts
what she sees.
I've no idea, no

Idea, no descriptive
tendency, no
numinous singular
from which I can
choose. . .

Only a translation,
impure, plural,
the cling of the world,
that-place-where
a verb's got to do.

THE SECOND PERSON

who sometimes had a face
                    and sometimes didn't,

who'd follow you home, carrying
                    in her hands several birds

as the sky wrapped around
                    a branch and ground a leaf black

and the horizon explained
                    itself behind the litter

and rain and bags
                    of leaves in the grass.

Sometimes you saw her balancing
                    along a curb at night,

holding the string you tied then
                    untied at the ends of vowels,

a thin thread you carry everywhere.
                    Sometimes she pulled back,

sometimes it tugged your stomach
                    and rose like a jewel in your throat.

Once, you saw the sky swallow paper-white birds,
                    then let them go,

tattered wing-edges in the sun.
                    They looked like fire. You thought,

they must be on fire, you thought
        she's waiting for me to explain this.

And when you couldn't,
       words fell at the ends

of your sentences. Her absence
       measured the weight of the room

like snow before it hits the
       grass, changing places in the wind,

brushing windows as windows
       wish, till it was time to go out,

lie down on the ground and erase
       the perfect angel.

NUDE

Does it scare you?
I ask my girls
who want me to
climb into the bath—
by which I mean,
You don't really
want to look
like me now
do you?
—as if their laughter
weren't part
of my question,
as if my question
were a dolphin
rising from
below, friendly,
miraculous—
as if I might
find out what I
am made of
by asking them.

OVER MY HEAD

Jerusalem

the call to prayer I used to mistake

for the prayer itself

wakes me. Then

there's the rug's gold-burgundy weave,

crown of spray and plume-like leaves

on the wall: a maze of eyes

like a peacock, or a flower, or a wine

glass overturned. My mistake,

not knowing this was made

for unfolding

onto the floor, for

the faithful bending

the dark hour,

for silence

turning to prayer.

AMONG THE MUSES

They're harmless,
Muse said to Muse.
They're not that great,
Muse said to Muse.
They're babies!
Muse said to Muse.
Devising poems,
Muse said to Muse.
Alone at night,
Muse said to Muse.
Banishing their demons,
Muse said to Muse.
What kind of demon?
Muse said to Muse.
You too, then?
Said Muse to Muse.

(Meir Wieseltier, 1966)

A MATTER OF TIME

Beach Camp, Gaza

Say one scalding
summer, you had 100 minutes

alone of electricity each day:

how would you use them?

Maybe you'd have
dinner by the LED,

or bring them to the sea,

shine figure 8's on the foam.
        But what if the water

nauseates?

        Bored at home,
would you let them out?

They're coming on, soon.

        Would you waste

what you've got for talk
        of failing sewage pumps?

        When you fall

asleep,
　　　　will they still
　　　　　　be yours?

Would you play with

them on your phone?
　　　　Would you share?

The drones care.

　　　　　　Say the sea
　　　takes them—

would that matter?

　　　　　　If someone calls

—who will answer?

NATIVITY

My dears,
I arranged that dark paradise
                    all for you,

knowing how much you love water,
careful to make sure
each pool was body temperature,
that the waves
                    rose with the waves,

and for your pleasure
included five small meals a day.
                    Now that you're here

you've, no doubt, come to question
the way out, a mystery that
could be solved only
by diving with your heads,
                    then your shoulders

and then, your hands.
It's the kind of probing
                    I'd love you

to love, our still life breaking open into life,
which won't permit you any distance.
Gone that innocence,
                    you know by now

there is no way out,
only an end
seeking a means
                    of living within.

MOTHER AND DAUGHTER ON A BENCH, REPLICA

Almost eleven, she says the Mars ice cream cone is so much like
the bar, she can barely tell the difference. It's a cool summer
evening, typical. She asks why people always call it beautiful.
Meir's just passed by—I hardly recognize him minus the hat. He
turns around, we talk, say goodbye and I search my phone for
his paintings. *I don't like it when people change it. I want people to
paint the exact tree,* she says. That a student today, twice her age,
said the same this morning, disappoints, but doesn't surprise.
She's leaning in, into the low light over the surface of the leaves,
now, through the window past the window of my screen. I don't
tell her what I told my students, only suggest that, perhaps, we're
bound to feel many things at once. I'd like to replicate this bench,
the breeze off her hair, her willingness, still, to sit here. But
mimesis ends where it begins. *What a beautiful night* is all I say.

TRANSLATING

One lives there where,
hearing a certain song,
she forgets it isn't native
on her tongue. Where words rise

to her throat, she doesn't
watch out the window and
stepping onto the porch at night,
she forgets. It's not native

to search out syllables,
collect minutes in a sieve.
She lives there where
she forgets. It's not native.

FIRST THING'S

—*to make the* person
        who'll write the poems,
the poet said—and, answering
        a question I
must have asked
        but can't recall: *You learn*
to live with your imperfect
        self—then went
back to her dinner,
        as if that were all.

from LOOKING AT A BEE

i.

In the square light of the window—
on the pane, from outside,
a bee's shadow
so slight you can hardly see her wings.

She's on her back.
Narrow.
Six thin legs—
exposed
and bare,
an ugly threat,
the bee crawls.

How will we crown her in poetry?
What would you propose?
A little boy will come and announce:
the queen—she has no clothes.

ii.

In the sunlight, she was a golden leaf falling,
in the blossom, a dark drop of honey,
in a swarm of stars, a bead of dew—
and here, she is shadow.

A single word in the whirring swarm,
urgent news in the lazy summer heat,
the play of light in twilight's dusty glow—
and here, she is shadow.

(Leah Goldberg, 1964)

ii.

RIDDLE

Who has wisdom hidden
        deep inside, who
            makes the heart discern?

Who colors the skies
        lapis with wisdom, who
            tilts the pitchers of heaven?

Do you know how dust
        solidifies, and how
            clods of earth amass?

Do you hunt the lion's
        prey and can
            you satisfy his craving

as he crouches in his
        den, poised
            to ambush from the thicket?

And who gives the
        raven its prey when its young
            cry out to God

wandering about—
        without
            a thing to eat?

(from Job 38)

BESIDE HERSELF

she is, our youngest.
                        She speaks of faces
          revolving in turnstiles,

heads between bars chucked live

from severed necks

onto the assembly line. Wings. Feathers.
Knock-kneed tossed into the packing area

                  as if out of the air—

there are laws that forbid this, religious and otherwise.

Precisely at the point when you begin to develop

a conscience, you must find yourself
at war with your society.

But there are bunkers

                  I don't want to be in.

                  Please, if you kill them,
             don't use those machines.

She's learning to read.

In the video she wasn't meant to see, metal poles
through ribs. Wings slapping
snapped necks.

The law, like her, couldn't care less how pure your heart.

> *Please use machines that don't hurt—*
she dictates for the letter we write.

And that is why my daughter is lucky.

When you see the naked, the prophet says, *clothe them.*

> He doesn't say: feel bad.

The law she lays down
is transitive: *Don't hurt.*

The children worked, slowly, carefully, leaning over the chocolate iridescence. They knew I knew—breakfast would be cake. He funneled his hands for the sprinkles, she poured the letters through—*Mazal*. There wasn't room for *Tov*. They tried to fix it. *Where will the Good go*, they asked. In their language, *Luck* + *Good* = *Congrats*. They could have half. They took it.

TRANSPARENT

First,

        silence is so accurate.

Yet, I wonder:

the kids' room at night,

          stilled

by their breathing weaving the air—

            isn't *that*

the precision I'm after?

~

Take this morning,

        the bath's ledge:

    Cinnamal,

        Vanilla Planifolia,

Ylang Ylang,

        Cocos Nucifera, now

and then Limonene,

essence of Geranium,

           Rosemary Leaf,

Aqua,

           Steam—

        ~

Or the instant

someone long

gone I love

glides into the room

on a wave of perfume—

and I remember the Hebrew

word for *scent*, ריח *(rey'ah)*—

differs by

just one letter

from *spirit*, רוח *(ru'ah)*—

as though a single

strand of the *Yud*

had nestled down

inside the middle *Vav.*

O HELICOPTER

Jerusalem

stirring the clouds
          above,
      charged with thwarting

threats with no
         aim other
      than our safety

and protection
         (this election):
      arranging

the air again and
         whirring
      in our ear

there's nothing
         we can do, O
      nothing, with a

sigh, you
         and your friends
      on high (and I).

THE DEMOLITION ORDER

Al Walaja

which comes

out of nowhere, arranging
         her face,

a window into which people look
(though *don't see*—

arranging changing placing

         a perhaps paper in her hand,
a strange
thing *Can you* (and known)

       read this here
changing everything carefully

—*she can't quite believe.* It's like

a Hand in a window

(she herself can read
the writing

carefully to and fro moving
Old things
         on the wall) while
         the words

stare, *with no reprieve through*
                freshly cut windows

moving a perhaps
fraction of a flower here,

        the bulldozer dropping her
tiles, fixtures

                        in a pile of crushed

        cement and jasmine (*an*
inch of air),

room atop
room,
                        while my friend

whose home it
is again, who throws

        her head back when she laughs,

                whose daughters are watching her—

sets *the long plastic table* for dinner without
breaking anything.

LINES FROM IBN EZRA

What am I and what is my life, what
is my fortitude, my power?

Chaff in the wind, for You
who know my every flaw.

POEM AT WAR

Gaza and Jerusalem

i.

The world minds
for awhile, is
dismayed, (dismay
a momentary stay
against
the world's
minds mining
the words they
make from
that which is
at stake
for us, O Lord,
says a friend on
the other side
of the

ii.

line): the world
loves
what it knows,
it glows
in droves
of pharmacies,
walls of balms
to no end,
the mystery
of this so-called
calm we bend
these sides
of the line.
The lines.

ABOUT YOUR NEW PLACE

For the Jewish settlers moving into Palestinian homes in Sheikh Jarrah, East Jerusalem

The bathroom door won't close.
I held it shut for my daughter.
          The walls are a thick plaster

and should keep out the rain,
          except for a hole in one
corner plugged with Play-Doh.

Near the square, before or after
the protests, you'll find a slide where
          your kids might play. . .

When we knocked,
          the father insisted—stay.
Oh that's all right, we said.

He left the pan on the flame,
poured onto a plate a bag
          of powdered sugar. Now

that you're moved in,
          you'll want
to cover up the flaws, but have yet

to conjure the likes of those pastries,
the last whiff of which was
          driven out in full

accordance with your laws.

A CERTAIN CORRESPONDENCE

makes things make sense, for instance,
      when the kids called out a name

through the lattice
      of our third-floor window, in unison,

hours before it happened, pointing
      to something just past their eyes,

their gazes relaxed, as if
      airborne apparitions were matters

of fact—while all *I* saw was the pine
      shaken by a breeze—and our friend was

no more than a name they knew
      from overseas. So when the phone rang,

I almost wanted to say—
      but held back as if it were news,

and the news made true
      not death, exactly, but something

about life, which we already knew.

BEYOND BELIEF

And then there's one hundred and three
        year-old Mazal, who half her life

cleaned bodies before burial.
Did they ever come back to you?

       No, she guffaws, proof of a job
well done. Only one:

during the eulogy, someone *saw something*.

Mazal opened the shroud.
I ascended, said the woman who'd died.

       They said I must come back.
Sometimes I tell this story as a test:

if you believe it, we can be friends.

It can help to visit
another realm, and not just

       the realm of the dead. I call
my sister, Mazal waves to a face before

realizing it's her own.

My sister's been crying. Mazal rounds
her arms: *you'll see how it grows!*

   —and now that I've come back
to tell her, she looks up

at the ceiling and laughs at what she knows,
she knows she knows.

A REVENANT

Memorial Day on the air, Jerusalem

i.

Fresh torches
are lit in the glow.
Beside the fallen,
our wildly successful
Prime Minister.
Eighty-two-year-old F.
(to whom I've come
to pay respects)
hollers *Bring out the popcorn!*
slapping the leg
under her long
nightgown.

ii.

So long as we mind
the rules, they'll light
another: mother
of this year's fallen
tells the story as
the girls dance
a slow remembrance
for the rest
of the class:
the flipped
tank run out of shells,
what could they have done,
chosen among
the chosen for
another year's song.

iii.

I dance with a boy.
Herein:
unfathoming
mother's
breast, herein
wingspan
of metal (mettle,
mental)
winged bets cast.
I've made him.
Each year more
not less. Here, now,
my daughter's arabesque,
my rotten attitude.

iv.

Year after year
(son fell in '88):
how does she make
it through? *I stopped
knitting.* How?
Took up
Cooking. But...
I turn the page
and: *He visited!*
I'm here!
It wasn't a dream.
Can you imagine?
Just like him,
to show up like that
out of the blue.

SONGS OF JUNE 6, 1967: FROM A LETTER

Our love
was beautiful in the starlight.
The walls of our houses
were black in the starlight.
Your face
paled to thin silver
in the starlight.
Your sons
lie tonight
on sand that cools
in starlight.

(Leah Goldberg, 1967)

METAPHYSIC

If Prometheus wanted fire,

he should have ascended
        with Zeus and begged forgiveness
until the fennel-stalk filled with flame.

He should have entered the realm where
        the dead listen
and give counsel, should have taken
any advice rather than wait,

pinned to a frost-bitten cliff. No one
would have told him to fight
        like this.
Humble yourself, says Epimethus.

In the army, the hardest drill—

lie on the ground. Imagine loving
        a woman without your legs,
then without your arms or hands.

They'd just finished a long navigation.
You've never seen guys break down like that...
        That he'd imagined me
was meant to reassure, and it did.

If Prometheus had wanted fire
        he must have been
all of twenty, twenty-one, too

tired to lie there for long, too young
to conjure the impossible.

KNIGHTS AND HORSES

The knights' lances pierced the skies
and the horses burst with pride.

As for me, I drew tall, proud horses,
with no knights or swords.

Without reins, my horses went wild
on paper, floor, and walls.

Then, flung with me to the ground,
they sprouted wings.

And now, as they soar through the air—
I call up their memory here.

(Amir Gilboa, 1963)

DIAGONAL WINDS

Clementines near Beit Hanoun
with the children till drizzle
        glazes the bags we haul

back to the kibbutz. In Friday's paper,
        a group of professors
has published a half-page ad

        denouncing the Occupation.
One wants to go on record,
to declare: *I would never*—while what

she wishes is: *I'm not.*
I'm not one to stretch her legs
        across the couch, crouched

behind gray-and-white print.
        A storm, crash
and flash at once, scares the children

        to shelter. Not one who,
before going back to reading,
says it's only a storm in the West.

Next week we attend a demonstration.
A few days later,
        our sniper shoots Jamil's

brother through the head.
        The neighbors
across the yard are renovating;

the one next door has built
a garden of Qassam rockets
and old combines. Every few

summers, parents concede
the noise outside is not an act of God.
        My friend will spend

the night in a windowless
        room; his brother
will grunt himself to sleep

        while outside it pours
as everyone swore it would.
We smelled it in the air.

iii.

DAY OFF

I'm taking the day off from my longings,
from my years, my time and all the books that have ever
endeavored to teach me a world in exacting words.

And I like it—
pondering things, needing no answer.

What is the name of that tree? And how
does one sing a bird's silence? From where
has the wind carried that star?

And am I lost forever to
the prettiness of nearby things?
Or maybe what
is farthest off of all
will restore my soul?

(Leah Goldberg, 1967)

THE ORIGINS OF USELESS THINGS

If neither for,
nor so, nor
nought, not
even sought, and,
to be sure,
not ought—
then, what?

~

Maybe
to be needed
but not to need it.
To live
on behalf of,
like the curve
in discursive.
(By the letter?)
Not just
to name,
though this
often is
the claim.
I want more
and less: to do
what I
must and
(yet) to stay.
To be a stay?

~

What it means to be lucky:
time to do this, for one.
For *what?* Just now a lizard,
silver-blue striped,
crawled under the front flap
of Mahfouz's stories.
What does it find there?
The Time and the Place.

~

Rather than to name, to make. Better?
But what would that be?

And if it's knowable,
what is it we (hopeful) seek?

~

Care's root, in fact, belies
                    apprehension of evil, fear.

Is that how I want to live?

                    Make of yourself a home.

Of whom? *A home.*
                    Did you know, Annie,

the ancient graft of *hospitality*

                    held in its helix

all three tendrils:
                    host, stranger, guest? In a word,

what will *you* make of *that*?

IDEOLOGICAL

I saw a snail swallow whole a twig
and the twig slide
            down
        its snail-like body—for it was still
a snail though it had
swallowed something one could follow,
            it seemed, all the way
            down.

SUPERFICIAL

Leaves wind their way

        into the glass,

spring black

        or green. Morning,

                Middle C from a window,

     rain and rowboat,

            the lake fills

the surface and only—

        only then
                the depths.

BIRD OF THE AIR

The paper boat was dropped in the puddle
and the lake filled with birds.
The bird plucked her extraneous wings,
ripped out her beak and licked the blood
from the open wound: new lips. Finally, she said,
I've arrived. The stench of burnt grass, bits of thistle,
baked earth, a weak trickle of water,
body-temperature. The vague glimmer in the haze
is the sun, the bird explained. Time to get to work,
to build a city and a tower, its head in the sky.

(Meir Wieseltier, 1994)

SUMMER PROJECT

Worst was the butterfly's wings lapping
against the jar, a nervous chorus
brushing and missing,
brushing and missing
the edge of glass:
if it saw, it saw cold

wet grass climbing the edge,
the blue-brown wing
on a finger of bark,
orange-blue, in the sky at sunrise:
worst was how, tacked to cardboard,
it hung and fell

and the children placed it on
the sidewalk under glass
until fire hit
and burned through its seams,
lines breaking body from wing: worst was
lifting stones,

looking for the clear-winged one
who pulsed over bushes
anywhere it liked,
through the yard past the pine
into the weeds,
brushing rain

off a leaf, catching light in the net.

LAZIZ THE TIGER TRANSFERRED FROM WORLD'S WORST ZOO

Khan Younis, Gaza

Beginings are hard, he scrawled in the sand. *Never give up,* his mother said. Sometimes he saw *the keeper stuffing dead pelicans.* Once, it was a monkey. Sometimes, with all that sawdust, *he found it hard to breathe.* He had a cross breeze, the bars, the call to prayer, black eyes, *an enviable BMI.* With good grades *plus some bureaucratic luck,* there was immigration. Once, when he woke, *a white deer with fresh black stripes appeared.* The children had wanted a zebra; *it made them feel* like they were in a *real zoo.*

BIPED

A peculiar creature, the biped—
in the flesh, he's just another
predator, except that
he alone cooks and curries his prey;
he alone wears animals
and turns them into shoes;
he alone believes
he is a stranger, he alone protests
his fate, he alone laughs,
and even more wondrous—
only he is willing
to ride a motorcycle.
He has ten fingers,
two ears,
a hundred hearts.

(Dan Pagis, 1975)

OF THE EYE

Trace your finger along
            your eyebrow
toward your ear against
the outer ridge of bone:

if you slipped your hand
beneath you'd find
            the lacrimal gland,
which sends droplets over

the cornea, making
            a thin film, then
draining through the
puncta, two apertures

under the lids.
As for abnormal secretions,
            when, for instance,
they spill and spill

onto the cheeks—
            these people are far
easier to treat
than those whose flow

is weak. Still,
I can't answer
            what you really
want to know,

which, if I'm right,
            isn't how
they fall, but how
we carry them, just so.

STRAYS

Follow it, they say,
though it does
take you, really,
you and your
will out of its way.

~

Was it a spirit?
Why does it matter?
After Anna died, the scent of her home—

cedar, quilts, a whiff of must—
overwhelmed my
room. *Hi,* I said, or asked, into the absence,

which, it seems, she defied.

~

White finery,
petals fluttering as though
no one else were here—
I, too, will disappear
into the window of this mirror.

~

Fresh and flush
     from some other
embrace, how here how far how
     nearly you are,
neonate, encased.

from POEMS WHERE THE ROAD ENDS

Teach me, Lord,
                    to bless and pray before

the secret of a withering leaf,
the glow of ripening fruit,

this freedom to behold, feel, exhale;
                    to know, to wait, and fail.

Teach my lips a blessing, a song of praise
in the freshness of your hours

morning and evening,
                    so my day, today, won't seem

like any of the others
or subside into routine.

(Leah Goldberg, 1955)

THE COLOR OF LIGHT

Over a doorway, the wooden floor
seems wet with it, a color named for its presence
though not a color, exactly: surface
on sidewalks, roofs, chandeliers,
an orchid's petals, meaning less-than:
light blue, light green, light taste,
tree-trunks rising in a canopy
it falls from, shedding on streets
and desks in quiet rooms, a hospital bed,
one button for the nurse,
the other to read,
inside of a hazelnut, coconut's grain
cumulus clouds, hills of air,
the ballerina leaping-as-air,
a stage before the show, house lights up,
mouths in conversation, white teeth,
something left unsaid:
                          Let there be
laughter tumbling down a stairwell,
the film that covers the eye that turns
to meet it, the lacquer, till it dries.

LINES FROM A CENTO

But haven't you noticed
beauty's fallen out of fashion?
Thrown in the sun's descending car,
it will do as it wishes,
will land like the peacock not ready
for splendor. O ever-pleasing Solitude,
companion of the wise and good,
have I spent too much, or not enough,
of my life on this? There have been, granted,
other things: duty, devotion—
vows cast to the earth,
taking root as seeds and sutures.
All my love I've asked: what's this?
All my life, these topographical errors.

PHEROMONAL

Coming home,

        first thing,

I take in the

lakes. And since

        I've been gone so long,

           all I need

is to lie

back on my parents' lawn,

        and the whole blue city wafts

up from the green,

green grass.

SYNTAX

Do you pray, a girl asked her mother

in a dark room.

        I wish I could say

what she said—

    My life's a prayer—

           and mean it,

      because she did, and it was.

and sometimes grandeur

            gives rise

to the simplest clause.

SOLICITATION

A few things:

> gold-flecked,

> > myrrh and scrim,

> chicory and birds

dappled or dipped in ink,

> > > a place I can stay—

> people, leaves that want

> > to meet the wind,

green things brooding—

> > > the life

> > and its perfection, though

> > > only one of them

> > > > makes a sound.

> Stick around, they seem to say

> > > from the air,

or from a prayer that goes on

                    making room, and a room

         where things hang, for a spell.

GHAZAL FOR TWO

I don't know how to look for You,
or me and you, the me that's You.

You're in the details, it's true—
and *True*'s one of the names we call You,

but that must be found, and only by the few
who wait *without* looking for You.

Soon the blossoms will imbue
my room with the aroma of You,

unraveling back to that view
they say belongs to You

and birds will come, taking their cue
and my window again will fill with You,

and in their thrall, I'll confuse
myself with the sound of You

and know the things I shouldn't do
and do them anyway with You.

For us it's nothing new,
nor is this form, which will have to do

until it breaks (with birdsong)
through a window into You.

THE ORIGINS OF USELESS THINGS

I Have Not Caused Hunger, I Have Not Caused Weeping—

an ancient prayer, an admonishment from afar?

Knowing it will never be true. . . All we've got, it seems,

is what we *do* do. To be: transitively—you.

NOTES

A CONVERGENCE

Cf. Online Etymology Dictionary (www.etymonline.com), from which many of the definitions were paraphrased or quoted.

NATIVITY

This poem takes its initial cues from Stephen Dunn's "A Bowl of Fruit."

BESIDE HERSELF

"Precisely at the point when you begin to develop a conscience, you must find yourself at war with your society." Cf. James Baldwin's "A Talk to Teachers."

"When you see the naked, clothe them": Cf. Isaiah 58:7.

TRANSPARENT

"Silence is so accurate": Attributed to Mark Rothko.

THE DEMOLITION ORDER

This poem is indebted to e.e. cummings' "Spring is like a perhaps hand" and tells of a friend from al-Walaja, a Palestinian village located between Jerusalem and Bethlehem, where many homes and other structures are under threat of demolition by the Israeli authorities.

BEYOND BELIEF

There is a tradition in Judaism to go to tsadikim, righteous people, for blessings.

THE COLOR OF LIGHT

"The lacquer, till it dries": Cf. Tomaž Šalamun's poem, "Lacquer."

LINES FROM A CENTO

The third, sixth and seventh lines of this poem are derived from a cento ("Throned in the Sun's descending car") composed by Wordsworth, which, in his preface, he attributes to Mark Akenside and James Thomson, respectively.

ACKNOWLEDGEMENTS

Grateful acknowledgement is extended to the editors of the following publications, in which many of these poems appeared, sometimes in earlier versions or under different titles:

The Adirondack Review: "Of the Eye," "Transparent," "Solicitation"

The American Literary Review: "Translating"

ANMLY: "Laziz the Tiger Transferred from World's Worst Zoo"

The Art of Poetry, ed. Christine Perrin, Classical Academic Press, 2012: "Nativity."

Atticus Review: "Nude"

Barrow Street Review: "Summer Project"

Bennington Review: "Diagonal Winds"

Birmingham Poetry Review: "About Your New Place" and "Metaphysic," "O Helicopter"

Born Magazine: "The Second Person"

Canon: "The Color of Light"

Gulf Coast: "Beyond Belief" and "The Demolition Order"

The Journal: "Day Off" and "Over My Head"

The Koren Tanakh, The Magerman Edition, (Job 38:36-41), Koren Publishers, 2021: "Riddle."

Literary Imagination: "Neonate" (Cf. "Stray")

Matter Monthly: "A Convergence" and "What It Means To Be Lucky"

On the Seawall: "Poem at War"

The National Poetry Review: "Beside Herself"

Painted Bride Quarterly: "Lines from a Cento"

Plume: "Cling of the World"

Plume Poetry Anthology No. 9, ed. Daniel Lawless, Canisy Press, 2021: "Mother and Daughter, Replica"

Rattle: "A Matter of Time"

Saint Katherine's Review: "Ghazal for Two," "Syntax"

Smartish Pace: "A Certain Correspondence," "Strays," "Looking at a Bee"

Seventy Sacred Hebrew Songs, ed. Yair Harel and R. Roly Matalon, Global Piyut Music, 2023: "Lines from Ibn Ezra" (from Avraham Ibn Ezra's piyyut, "Lord My Longing Is Yours").

Verse Daily: "Beside Herself"

With This Night, by Lea Goldberg, trans. Annie Kantar, University of Texas Press, 2011: "Looking at a Bee."

Acknowledgement is also extended to the following publishers, authors and their estates for permission to publish translations from the Hebrew of the following:

Goldberg, Lea. "Yom Chofesh," *Shirim*, volume C, p. 272. Tel Aviv: Sifriat Poalim, 1973.

Goldberg, Lea. "Shirei Shisha beYuni 1967" Poem A (Mitoch Michtav), *Shirim*, volume C, p. 279. Tel Aviv: Sifriat Poalim, 1973.

Goldberg, Lea. "Histaklut biDvora," *Shirim*, volume C, p. 44-45. Tel Aviv: Sifriat Poalim, 1973.

Goldberg, Lea. "Shirei Sof haDerech," Poem C (Lamdeini, Elohai), *Shirim*, volume B, p. 154. Tel Aviv: Sifriat Poalim, 1973.

Gilboa, Amir. "Susei haParashim." *Kechulim veAdumim,* p. 209. Tel Aviv: Am Oved, 1963.

Pagis, Dan. "Du-Regel," *Kol haShirim,* p. 197. Tel Aviv and Jerusalem: Hakibbutz haMeuchad and Mosad Bialik, 1991.

Wiesltier, Meir. "Of haShamayim," *Machsan*, p. 49. Tel Aviv: Hakibbutz haMeuchad, 1995.

Wieseltier, Meir. "Sicha bein Muzot," *Kitzur Shnot haShishim*. Tel Aviv: Hakibbutz haMeuchad, 1984.

Annie Kantar's work has appeared in *The American Literary Review, Barrow Street, Bennington Review, Birmingham Review, Cincinnati Review, Gulf Coast, Literary Imagination, On the Seawall, Plume Anthology 9, Poetry Daily, Poetry International, Rattle, Smartish Pace, Tikkun, Verse Daily,* and elsewhere. Her translation from the Hebrew of *With This Night*, the final collection of poetry that Leah Goldberg published during her lifetime, appeared with University of Texas Press (2011), and was shortlisted for the ALTA Translation Prize. The recipient of an Academy of American Poets Prize and a Fulbright Scholarship, she recently published her literary translation of *The Book of Job* (Koren, 2021).

CPSIA information can be obtained
at www.ICGtesting.com
Printed in the USA
JSHW082331110623
42981JS00002B/139